Ch
Futures

South Tees

Edited by
Helen Aitchison

Write on the Tyne

First published in Great Britain in 2025 by Write on the Tyne CIC.

Printed and bound by Amazon

Paperback ISBN: 9781739488291

Cover image: by Paul
For my beloved son Ryan, whom I painted for every day of my sentence.
All my love, your dad, Paul xx

Published by Write on the Tyne
www.writeonthetyne.com

Foreword

The South Tees Changing Futures Programme was established in 2021 to improve outcomes for adults facing multiple disadvantages, such as homelessness, substance misuse, mental health challenges, domestic abuse, and interactions with the criminal justice system. It aims to stabilise and improve individuals' lives, transform local services, and test new approaches to funding and accountability. We are one of fifteen local partnerships funded by the UK Government and the National Lottery Community Fund until March 2026.

This collection of experiences is a way of sharing stories so that we can learn from lived experiences to influence the development of our programmes, celebrate success, and challenge stigma. The creativity, determination, and positivity are empowering.

Whilst we continue to make great strides, there is still much more to do.

Mark Adams, Chair of the South Tees Changing Futures Board and Joint Director of Public Health for South Tees

Contents

A Painting 1
A Welcome 2
Acceptance 3
Albert Park 4
Being a Prisoner 5
As One 9
Asking for Help 10
Be Proud 11
Butterflies 12
Cloud 9 13
Days Like This 14
Days Like This 15
Dear Rachel, aged 6 (1982), ... 16
Demon of Ink 18
Do Good 19
Don't Judge 20
Feeling Welcome 21
Fight Together 25
Finding Myself 26
Flowers 28
Freedom 37
Freedom 38
Give and you Shall Receive 39
Going Home 40
Growth 41
Happiness 42
Hart Gables 43
Hart Gables 44
Hart Gables 45
Help 46
Holy Saturday 47
Home 48
Hope 49
Hummingbird 50
I Changed my own Chemistry 52

I will be me 53
Imagine 54
Jailer 55
Justice 56
Light After Dark 57
Light After Dark 60
Long Sentence 61
Lost and Found 64
Make a Person Welcome 65
Mental Health and Me 66
Moonlight 67
Mum's Advice 68
My Colourful Garden 69
My Community 70
My Great Folk 71
My Home 72
My Story 73
Nature's Night Light 75
Never Leave our Love 76
New Beginnings 77
No Reason 79
No Shame 80
Number One 81
Ode to Neo 82
One Life 83
Our Middlesbrough 84
People Care 87
Positive Impact 88
Power to Change 89
Put it on the Slate 90
RC 92
Reach Out 94
Sam's Story 95
Seagull 96
Sharing 97
Soulmates 98
Standing Together 99
Straining for Hope 100

Strength in Together 101
Support 102
The Inner Struggles and Strength of Just 103
One Person 103
The Report 106
The Truth Shall Set You Free 107
Time Was 108
Together 109
Together, we can 110
All be Together 111
Together we are Stronger 112
Train Station 113
Unheard 114
Vessel 115
Walking Inspiration 116
Warm Welcome 117
Welcome 118
Welcome, my Friend 119
What is Important? 120
Art Work 121
Acknowledgements 122

A Painting

I painted a dystopian picture.
There on the broken cobbles, a twisted figure sprawls.
Is it man or woman? Is it even human?
Their umbilical cord bleeds.
Volcanoes erupt.
Clouds of fire and dust roll and scat across the tortured sky.
The sun glares harsh.
And there, almost hidden, a blade of grass pushes through the cobbles.
Even in the bleakest, most monstrous world, a blade of grass reaches for the light.
I call the painting, 'Hope'.

Alan

A Welcome

Welcome means,
I hope you are well.
So come into my space,
even if you're not well.
You are more than welcome to tell.
For to me, welcome means,
come into my love.
The love that was given to me,
straight from above.
I know this to be true.
For no matter where you go,
or what you do.
A welcome to someone,
or they to you,
means love is all around.
And all is safe and sound.

Cecilia

Acceptance

We live in a society where we are guarded by laws. Where sometimes you can't be yourself. People look down on you, maybe because of your beliefs, or because you feel you were born differently.

Being yourself can be a challenge but we all have the right to be ourselves. We all want to be accepted and left to live how we choose to live.

Sadly, we live in a society full of judgement and if you don't fit the mould, you can be frowned upon. Why is it so difficult for people to accept who you are and let you be you?

Craig

Albert Park

Crisp misty morning.
Crocuses, squirrel, ducklings.
The sun dares to shine.

Alan

Being a Prisoner

As a prisoner, my body and mind are confined by restricted freedoms as a punishment for breaking the law. The concrete and steel of the prison restricts my movements and the rules and regulations restrict my choices, behaviours, thoughts, and freedom of speech. For myself personally, the concrete and steel are just a temporary punishment compared to the lifelong emotional punishment that I have handed down to myself — due to the pain and damage I inflicted on my family, following a complete mental breakdown.

Art provides an escape and has therapeutic benefits. While my body and mind are restricted by the concrete and steel and often dysfunctional rules and regulations of the criminal justice system, my creativity is only restricted by my artistic ability and imagination. I have always been a creative person and began drawing as a child and studying music, which continued into adulthood to varying levels of commitment. It was only recently that I began to let go and experiment with my artwork. I'll never be a master artist, but I've begun stepping outside of my comfort zone and trying different techniques and nurturing ideas.

Early in my ten-year sentence, as a therapy for my mental health recovery, an occupational therapist in HMP Durham's Integrated Support Unit encouraged me to use creativity as a distraction. Prisoners noticed my talent and one asked me to freehand copy an image of a Japanese-style lion. He suggested that I could make an income drawing pictures for other prisoners, which would later lead to creating birthday cards, humorous images of other prisoners, large paintings, and tattoos.

While my sentence has meant that I am separated from my children and wife, art has given me the ability to create gifts for them. I began by freehand copying their favourite cartoon characters and then began creating storybooks for them. Every Christmas, I create my own Christmas cards, which I design to enable the cards to be placed in any order to create a Christmas scene.

During appointments with restorative justice, the case manager Becky, would visit my wife and children, who showed her pictures that I had made for them. An opportunity emerged with a chance to display artwork relating to lived experience in an exhibition in Middlesbrough called Mind Over Matter. Becky asked if I would be interested in taking part in the project. Following an appointment with the project manager, Ruth, it was explained to me that the project could be an opportunity to raise awareness of the prison system and prisoners' experiences. I shared several potential ideas that I had been working on, which both Ruth and Becky were impressed with. Ruth kindly supplied some materials and I began working on two of my ideas, which I felt more

confident were relevant and the best ideas.

One piece which I named **Identity** was a collage of sorts using coloured pencils, pen, and water paints, which portrays key moments in my life from my childhood through to the future. The images are a blend of positive and negative occurrences that formed my interest, identity, and my path in life.

Sea of Crisis was the other piece that I included and was an idea that I had held in my mind for over ten years. The idea came about when I had been contemplating the difficulties that I was facing with depression and drug addiction. I had explained the artwork idea to my GP and described that the isolation I felt was similar to being alone at sea during a storm, and in the distance, I can see a lighthouse which has shown me the direction I need to go in my mind. A poem was emerging from the waves next to an image of a man in a rowing boat. When I completed the piece, I was not completely happy with it, as it did not fully capture the detail in my mind. But it turned out better than I had expected.

After the exhibition in Middlesbrough ended in February 2024, Becky believed that one of my other ideas, which I had not originally submitted, was relevant to the Mind Over Matter project as it described the experiences of a prisoner within the UK prison system serving a long custodial sentence. I initially thought that the idea was too political and complicated, and I didn't believe it would fit in with the exhibition, as it is essentially an A4 page with no colours and lots of words. However, I decided to complete the piece ready for a second exhibition in Redcar.

Long Sentence is minimalistic and reminds me of John Lennon and Yoko Ono's artwork. The piece contains a long, unbroken sentence without full stops or commas, which explains the political and punitive reasons for longer custodial sentence tariffs. It also explains the difficulties, risks, and failures that the prisoner faces when serving along custodial sentence — due to the overpopulation, violence, underfunding, and lack of rehabilitation within the UK prison service.

The handwritten sentence is intentionally long to replicate the confusion, disorientation and lack of meaningful structure within long custodial sentences. The piece ends with a rhetorical question to prompt readers to contemplate and consider the practicality, purpose, and impact of the failures of the criminal justice system, long custodial sentences, and the UK prison service — which impacts prisoners and the community, as the focus of prisons lean too heavily on punishment and not enough on rehabilitation and reformation.

The **Long Sentence** piece was well received by the exhibition and even the probation service, who are planning to use the piece as a training tool to help probation officers understand the perspective of prisoners. When I entered prison in 2021, art was a hobby and therapy which later led to trading opportunities. I wonder how many artists have been paid for their artwork with haircuts? I had never considered that my artwork would be displayed in exhibitions and used as a training tool by the probation service.

Art will not build houses, feed the hungry and poor, or end conflict, but art can liberate the mind and enable expressive thought. It can portray an idea and spread a message, and bring people together. So, if anyone ever says that art is useless, remember that if you ever end up in prison, it could gain you some haircuts.

Anthony

As One

One day, the sky turned blue and fish swam in the ocean.
The sun, it shone on you, and life stood to attention.
All across the world had changed, things we knew were not important.
Life was different in exchange; nature back to set example.
We will find a way; it will come the day.
We will all stand tall; all be together.
Through the dark and light, we will sacrifice.
Fight the fight; all be together.
In this changing world of ours, love will conquer.
Now and forever, let our hearts and voices sing.
Free the spirits, float like a feather.
Love and unity in community.
Will all stand strong; all be together.
Friends and family will dance happily.
All stand tall; all be together.
All be together as one.

Mel

Asking for Help

It does not make it alright to cry all the time. Sometimes, they are happy tears. Sometimes, sad tears. Like when I woke up that morning, screaming and crying for my mam and dad. I got out of my bed and I needed help. I was taken to St Barnabas Church by two kind people.

One took me to Hope Foundation, now my safe place where I can be with friends. I am glad I came to the group. I just need to tell myself that I love myself. I know I am right to ask for help.

Margaret

Be Proud

The world can be hostile.
Scams, trickery, robberies, and assaults.
Abuse against women, knife crime.
Homophobic behaviour against LGBTQ+ people.
Why?
All people want is to be accepted for who they are.
We are *all human,* no matter our colour, sexual orientation, or anything else.
Be who you want to be.
Stand up, be proud of who you are.

Craig

Butterflies

When I first heard about Cloud 9, I had nervous butterflies, but I was told someone I know could come with me. My butterflies were less nervous and they had an edge of excitement, as if it might be okay.

When we entered the room, people turned but they were smiling. This made me feel welcomed and safe. I saw lots of different people, but everyone smiled. And they smiled with their eyes shining and hearts caring.

I felt at home. My butterflies were smiling and dancing.

Rae, Kane, Louise

Cloud 9

Caring

Lovely

Opportunities

Understanding

Delightful

9/9

Rae, Louise, Leo

Days Like This

I think I am old enough now to look back at my life and see where the good days had sadness and the bad days brought a life of the spirit; something to make you cry and something to make you smile. And through it all, I was never completely alone, even when I thought I was.

The days when I go and see my brother — now in a care home with advanced Alzheimer's — puts me on a downer. He was such a comedian, to the point where it would annoy me sometimes, because he even turned serious things into a joke. But he was right. It's how he dealt with his 'days like this'. And what better way: making jokes and using word-play. It seems to be all about how we think, negatively or positively.

What I do for him now, as he looks at me with a vacant stare, no one home, is hold a great big Magnum ice cream lolly in front of him and so far, he always reaches out and takes it from me. He downs it in a flash. Then I play him Buddy Holly on my phone and his legs start moving to 'Peggy Sue'.

Two years ago, he came after me down his driveway and told me to look after myself, and gave me the biggest hug.

He said, 'We all end up in the same place, you know?'

He was thinking of me and thinking ahead and trying to ease my days like this. This comedy was not ignorance, it was a mechanism for his days like this. God bless him.

Cecilia

Days Like This

You know what? There are days just like this.
Acceptance is the key.
Resistance brings on the misery.
Letting go and trusting, doesn't set us all free.
Life ain't always easy, sometimes, it's tough.
A skill, we're all learning; take the smooth with the rough.
Sometimes, we awaken and bounce out of bed.
Sometimes, it feels like we'd rather be dead.
But life is a gift, let's remember this truth,
slow down, smell the roses. Stop living on the hoof.
Adventures await us each and every day.
Make hay while the sun shines, let go the dismay.
Some days we'll struggle, we all know this is true.
But even when it's raining, the sky is still blue.
Beyond the clouds that seem to obscure the sun,
Still exists a world more playful and fun.
So yes, of course, take the rough with the smooth.
Life is a mystery, but doubts we remove.
We need the black threads as well as silver and gold,
to discover the riches our lives will unfold.

Terry

Dear Rachel, aged 6 (1982),

I wanted to write to you to let you know that life gets better, beyond your wildest dreams, in many ways, that right now, are actually not legal. You're going to struggle with friendships as you're all or nothing. Some people might say intense. But when you love, you love with all your heart.

Education will be difficult because your brain is so wrapped up in surviving. All your energy goes into not being you and managing how you think and feel. You'll come into your own, academically, in your thirties and forties. Keep going with it though, it's worth it. Drama will save your life, literally!

Right now, the world is divided into pink and blue with two genders. You will feel you didn't fit anywhere. You'll find yourself being attracted to women and not men, but you won't understand this until you move out and go to college. This is where your world expands and you learn about sexuality. You know deep down that you are gay but you find yourself scared of the repercussions for your family.

You never wanted to disappoint, and you'll go to self-sacrificing means to get through. Hold on though, because you'll find inspiring, understanding people who are compassionate and will guide you through this rollercoaster. Some will be friends, lovers, and therapists.

By the end of the 1990s, Labour will be in government and they will bring in the new laws for same-sex partnerships and for gay people to foster and adopt. This changes your life dramatically. After a few awful relationships, you'll end up married to an amazing woman, Sam, who you know instantly is your person. She'll love you for you, and you'll both be brave and courageous together, all the while through adoption and fostering.

Your boy, Matt, will steal your heart but drag you to the edge many times! He will grow to be an amazing, respectful man who loves both his mums deeply. You need to know that life is going to knock you sideways at times, but you will always, always get through. So much so that you'll use your negative experiences to help others.

By the time you're in your late forties, you'll feel confident in who you are and will have had gender-affirming surgery to truly be a trans masc non-binary person. Be proud of you, listen to your gut feelings, and stay strong to who you are.

I love you, Rachel, you are amazing and beautiful. People feel better in your presence, never forget that.

Yours always,
Rae
xxx

Demon of Ink

Be careful what you think,
when you dance with the demon of ink.
A dark, horrid sludge foul stink.
Thoughts designed to push you to your brink.
They break and beat you down,
have you feeling like a clown.
So you pummel and punch the ground,
start to fall to where dark souls are found.
So you lean into the rage and create an obsession,
your heart and soul have got you second guessing.
No time to pause to catch your thoughts,
won't be long before you're brought to the floor.
Lashing out, crying, I want no more.
Fuck the world and everything in it.
I no longer care, my thoughts, feelings, dreams; bin it.
I can't finish what the universe has planned for me.
I fall to my knees, hara-kiri.
Stop, hold your hand from the sword,
reach out for help, something we can all afford.
It is not weak to say, 'I need help,'
for demons and darkness, we all have felt.
No one should battle or fight alone,
my demon won't take me; you can't have my soul.
So build up, unite, together we will fight.
Unveil the darkness, destroy the demon.
If you need help; I no longer fear them, so neither should you.
Because with the right people, you'll beat yours too.

A Soul Saved

Do Good

We are stronger together when we have one common goal,
yes, we are!
We are stronger together when we have one common
agenda, yes, we are!

In a place where everyone is fighting for their own personal interests and selfish ambition and personality, it is not an easy thing to be stronger together. Black or white, we all have the same blood. In a place where power, money, and greed have enveloped the brain of the people, decision-making in a company, in the church, in the political systems, it is very hard to stay strong together.

But life is too short, so please try to do good.
Do to others what you want them to do to you.
Love your neighbour and love yourself.

Diana

Don't Judge

Don't judge a person on their appearance.
Not everyone is strong.
Some are vulnerable.
Nobody knows what's going on in their life.
Depression, anxiety, loneliness.
Don't judge unless you have walked in their footsteps.
Ask if they are okay.
Let them know you are there for a chat, a coffee, or a bit of company.
Sometimes, all we need is a friend to talk to.
Everyone is unique in their own way and deals with life the best they can.
Be a friend, not an enemy.
Love not war.
We are human, together.

Craig

Feeling Welcome

Welcome, I am finally discovering what this beautiful word means. Growing up in my house, I was the confident peacemaker and clown, repaid by also being the scapegoat, whipping boy, and omega.

The worst six months of my life finally broke me. The mind can be a dark place. It brought forth real demons in my head. But they were there to lead me to the light. Sometimes the biggest trauma turns out to be the greatest blessing. It guided me home to my true family. Born of spirit, not blood. Living with my soul sister, I truly know and understand the word. It is unity, belonging, and love.

Andrea

Welcome is a good word to me. When someone says welcome, it puts me at ease. I feel calm and happy to be there. Being made to feel welcome by a stranger is lovely. In a world that is being torn apart by crime and wars, it is hard to feel welcome in this world. So, meeting new people at groups where I have been made to feel welcome is what gets me through long days.

Tracy

It's not very often in my life that I've felt welcomed — that's mainly about me and not other people. General anxiety, shyness, insecurity, depression, social anxiety, and nerves. Meeting new people or going into new situations.

But although I am quite introverted, I do feel the need for social groups, events, and activities. Sometimes, I just want to

hide in a corner. Sometimes, I'm quite comfortable being surrounded by other people, but I don't actually interact. Other times, I seem very chatty, lively, and social. That can be a mask or diversionary tactic, or I genuinely feel included and connected. I feel welcomed here.
Alan

What is it to feel welcomed?
It is to be part of a group, to be accepted by all.
Feeling comfortable and relaxed.
Open door to all diversity.
Music brings happiness and welcoming vibes.
To feel welcomed gives a positive attitude of others,
offers friendship, support, camaraderie, love, and acceptance.
Julie

I feel welcome wherever I go. Whether it be at the Hope Foundation, 2B Creative, or at the choir. I'm a welcoming person to new or old friends, as learning is a new way to welcome love and compassion for others in our community and in our hearts. We don't have to be alone, as we are a welcoming community. So, I say welcome to everyone, new or old.
Sam

'You're welcome.' You hear it so often: after being served, opening a door, or doing a good turn for someone. Is it just a phrase now? Or do people really mean it? Is it an age thing? As the younger generation doesn't seem to use it at all.

How does it make you feel to hear it? I'm of an age where manners were as important as your school grades.

I like to be able to pass on a little bit of good will. You never know how important that little word is to someone. It may be the only pleasant thing they hear that day. It costs nothing, free to all. I like to feel it, so I hope to make someone feel it too. Life is hard and can be so daunting. So, do every little kindness you can — it is a blessing.

Marie

I felt unwelcome throughout my childhood and adolescence, even though I was told the door was always open. I know and knew that my shape wouldn't fit through the doorframe that was said to be open to me.

Growing up in the 80s and 90s, I was unable to see anyone who was like me. Only towards the end of the 90s did I witness new laws for my community to start to be legally welcomed in this country. Whilst being aware that many others still are unable to be themselves and feel welcome in their country, region, and homes.

I am still not fully welcome as a trans non-binary person in this country. However, there are places and people where I have felt incredibly welcome for who I am and safe to be me. Having never felt welcomed, those safe places mean the world to me. They are precious and help me to build a stronger me. I am grateful for sitting at the welcome table.

Rae

I feel welcomed when people are happy to have me in their company. When there is no judgement or negativity about me. Feeling inclusion, no matter what.

We are all human, no matter what. Everybody is welcome, to express themselves.

Craig

Welcome is a common language used in most places. Feel well when you hear welcome. Welcome to my world of excitement. You are welcome to my group. I feel welcome when I am in the midst of people, then I know the value of things and places.

Welcome is a unique word to use in a place where there is respect. You can be welcome in a family or at any place at any time, and in a safe place. One thing people should know is that not everyone who says welcome to you, really welcomes you.

Not everyone who smiles at you really welcomes you. Humans should welcome you, whatever comes their way, in good faith. Here, you are always welcome.

Diana

Fight Together

I often compare people to ants.
It may sound strange, but why not?
One ant is so tiny and powerless.
But together, these defenceless insects can build a huge, civilised community, and big houses.
Man is created to do good.
If all people fight together for kindness, warmth, and love, then peace will win on our planet.
Yes, we must fight for people.
And we must be together.

Anna

Finding Myself

I have been in a coercive control relationship with my son's father. I had no say in the matter and he drove me away from friends and people I worked with, who I lost all contact with. I was naïve about my relationship at that time. I loved him and went along with what he wanted. During the relationship, bit by bit, my personality changed. I wasn't allowed to speak to friends, male or female and only allowed limited time with my parents. He accused my mother of interfering, which she didn't but was helping me.

I lost my confidence and sense of humour. The only positive thing that came out of the relationship was that I fell pregnant with my son. My ex managed to control my pregnancy: antenatal checks and visits to the hospital. When I was in labour, having an emergency C-section, he was complaining about having to wear scrubs to be with me.

To be honest, in hindsight, I was single becoming a mother. He kicked off with the midwife, doctor, and health visitor. I was very ill with postnatal depression. My mother came to help and he continued making problems with people trying to help me.

On one occasion, he threw me and my newborn son in a carrycot, out of the door. This was the start of our breakup and I had to make a stand. I did make a stand and we split up for good. I realised in hindsight that he controlled me and I moved back to my parents' home. He had done terrible things: putting me down, calling me a lazy, greedy glutton. I was so glad to get out of this relationship and be just me and my son, Max.

We've lived our lives, better off without him. Max has had no contact with his dad, who is no longer living in Middlesbrough. Now, both Max and I are happy. I'm confident and I got my sense of humour back. I made new friends and joined support groups. I'm happy to be myself and wouldn't let anyone control me ever again.

Julie

Flowers

When I was asked to write a submission for this book, I had originally intended to write a piece detailing the ways in which realising I was transgender had helped me become a better person; both to other people and in how I felt about myself. I wanted to write something that would help people understand the joy that comes from my existence, because a lot of what is written about us tends to portray us as a pathology — as broken people at best in need of fixing, or pitying, and at worst, in need of eradication. My hope was to give people an alternative view of what our experience can be like, to see the reasons we pursue transition and what it gives us as we achieve it.

But as of the time of writing, the supreme court of the United Kingdom issued a ruling which directly attacks the right of trans women to be protected by the law. And many of the elite elements of our society are mobilizing to capitalise on this, drawing up further attacks on our ability to be recognized as women, our access to gender segregated public facilities, our ability to live our lives without being subjected to the indignity and danger of being forced into men-only spaces. Something I think that most women can easily comprehend the fear of, and the degradation that they would feel if such a thing were forced on them.

So, I am not feeling very joyful at the moment. I find it very difficult right now to access the feelings I had intended to write about. I am presently spending a lot of my time trying to console, support, steady, and protect as many of my kindred as possible — especially my sisters. All of whom are fighting through feelings of fear for their futures, for their personal safety, for their state of their lives if legal protections and recognitions that they have built their lives around, are revoked at the whim of the state — driven largely by organisations and individuals who do not know what it is to live in precarity. Who are entrenched in positions of wealth and power and do not need to ever fear persectuion by the power they wield against others with impunity.

That is the primary effect of these efforts. To rob people of their joy. To make people feel afraid for their future and their well-being. To make them suffer. This is the effect that the people who are celebrating this decision are celebrating. The simple, spiteful cruelty of making another human being hurt. The behaviour of the schoolyard bully, of the petty tyrant manager, of the leering drunk who puts his hands wherever he feels entitled to. Our discomfort, pain, grief, and fear, is their pleasure, and any claim to the contrary is either a conscious lie, or born of a cultivated and cowardly unwillingness to look at the people they are hurting, for the purpose of better maintaining the illusion that they are not doing this to us.

The threat, here, is not just to us — although we are presently the primary target. But the effects of these attacks will hit other people too. What can be the logical end result of policing bathroom access? Any woman who does not look feminine enough is harassed in the bathroom? The tide of anti-trans panic has already led to an increase in this happening. Trans men well into their transitions are now required to use the women's facilities? The fundamental lie that all of this is predicated on, is that you can reliably tell whether someone is transgender by looking at them. Which is patently false. People falsely accuse others of being transgender all the time, usually women, and the women this happens to and the harassment they go on to receive, are simply considered acceptable collateral damage in service of possibly hurting trans people.

If the goal were to protect women, then this would surely be cause for reconsideration. But the goal is not that, the goal is hurting trans people. In the face of all of this, I look for community with my kindred. Not just other trans people, but people who for one reason or another, are gifted with the ability to see the failings of the normative world, and appreciate the outsider perspective — that sees clearly through the fog of bad ideas that say people must behave a certain way because of what genitalia they have, or because of chromosomes, or 'to preserve western civilization' or whatever the latest nonsense is.

People can choose how they behave. And people are not wrong to find the role assigned to them by society to be unfitting, and to seek a different role, a different presentation, a different way of being. And through modern technology and a simple extension of empathy, people who want that can live very happy lives. To want to take that away is nothing but senseless cruelty.

You can't 'fix' us. You can't make us not feel the way we feel, any more than you can pray the gay away. You can at best stuff us back in the closet. But that isn't for our benefit, it's for yours. We should not be made to suffer and stifle in bodies and clothes that smother us, that cage us and which feel utterly wrong. To accept that you are transgender is to accept that you can not live in the prison of your assigned role. To accept it is to live for however long it takes, trying desperately to accept the body you have and the role you've been given. Until eventually, you come to realise that some part of you — some ephemeral part which you can't touch or name or place — simply will not accept the body you have, and will not accept the expectation to perform the idiotic dance of your assigned gender.

But it *will* accept another body, another performance, another role. One outside of the limits of your assigned gender. It will not only accept that alternative, but it will be *happy* with it, happier than you ever thought it possible for a human being to be. All you really need to get there is for other people to understand and not treat you like filth for wanting that. The medical treatment helps too. It can make your body feel right to you every day of your life, without having to fight it. But what *really* makes transition possible is other people letting you do it. Accepting that you're still a person. That this is important to you, and wanting you to do what brings you happiness. You can give someone that. Anybody reading this, you can give people that. All you have to do is want to understand, want to accept and find kinship with others, to be a decent human being. And I promise you that your trans friends will love you like a sibling for that, because it is very hard for us to find people we can trust in this day and age.

There is no sense at all in demanding somebody live constantly at war with themselves. Constantly fighting against a part of themselves that will not change; that no power on earth can change. We deserve to live at peace with ourselves and in peace with other people. If this sounds like the same argument made for gay rights, then that's because it is. I don't know what makes me this way and I don't frankly give a damn. But I do know that I spent thirty-five years of my life trying to make it work without accepting this, and it didn't. It didn't work before I even had the concept of 'being transgender', which I did not really have explained to me until I met a trans girl at university. And I didn't really understand it even then either. It took me a very, very long time and exhausting every other option before I was able to open myself up to the possibility of accepting an alternate way of being, of conceptualising myself. But once I did that, everything clicked into place.

The world once viewed through a warped and broken glass became clear as a bright winter's day. The understanding that my difficulties with performing masculinity are not something I have to struggle with for the rest of my life, that I can simply *not be that at all,* was incredibly freeing. Men don't feel like this; if I was a man, then why would everything about it just feel stupid and wrong? Oh and if you're reading this and saying, 'Of course men feel like this. I feel like this all the time. It's part of being a man,' then all I can say is give it a few years and get back to me.

A lot of us struggle with the realities of becoming ourselves in a world that is very often hostile to our existence. And as with gay people, I think that when you are conditioned to see yourself as a pathology, as an aberration to be hidden away or corrected, it can make it extremely hard to see the positives of your nature. But this is again an imposition of an unjust world, it doesn't have to be like this.

Before I realised I was transgender, I realised I was bisexual. It took me until my twenties to figure that one out but once I did, and had a bit of time to grow into it, I came to see it as a blessing; something I treasure and am very thankful for. Pride is a good word for describing the act of being yourself, unashamed and openly. But I think my actual relationship with my sexuality is more accurately described as thankfulness, because through it I am given ways of perceiving and experiencing the world that other people are denied. It is a rare and precious gift, and I feel exactly the same way about being transgender.

A lot of my kindred have a difficult relationship with sexuality and gender, and it is true that we can sometimes be made to feel bad about ourselves because of them. And in the case of gender, a lot of that can feel quite self-generated; as if you were born to hate your body, cross-wired without your consent and having to spend your life undoing that damage. I would personally say that I think this, too, is put on us by social conditioning. But even if we just accept it as a fact of our experience regardless of where it comes from, that sense of conflict and unhappiness is made into a fleeting shadow by the transcendent experience of finally getting to be yourself.

Can you imagine what it's like to spend your life feeling like you are perpetually out of tune with everything? Like nothing quite works right. Existing while observed by others always feels wrong. You have to put on a facade in order to present the unconvincing semblance of humanity. And the effort of operating the stiff, stifling disguise you have to wear everywhere makes it utterly impossible to actually enjoy anything, or to find true connection with others. And you don't know why it feels like this. You just know that it's wrong. It won't stop being wrong; you can never learn, no matter how much you practice, to wear the costume fluently. It is always arduous and always sapping away your will to do anything, your will to even exist.

And then from that, one day, you realise you don't need to wear the costume at all. Sure, you've been wearing it so long that parts of it have become stuck to you, but for the first time in your life, you know you don't *need* to wear it; you aren't *supposed* to wear it. You take off the parts of it you can, as quickly as possible, and for the first time in your life, you can see the bright sun and breathe the clear air. You are alive and in true contact with the world around you, without the barrier of the false self getting in the way. You look in the mirror and for the first time in your life, you recognise yourself. There are still bits of the false self visible, of course, but you *know what you're looking for* now and you can see a path to get them off you. To let the person you recognise as yourself come out and be visible, to you and to everyone else.

Your life now has a clearer purpose than it ever has before. The task is a big one, yes, and it will require skill, commitment, practice, and sacrifice to achieve. But it is a *clear* task, one that is spoken to you from somewhere inside yourself that you cannot name or touch, but it speaks clearly and what it speaks makes more sense to you than anything you have heard in your life. And the burning, radiant, indescribable joy that each step along that road brings you, it has no comparison. It is something you can't properly describe. It feels like the first time you fell in love. It feels like a perfect summer day on a high hill, looking down into a beautiful forest valley with the breeze in your hair, the sound of birdsong, and the scent of heather in the wind.

Whatever else you do, as long as you keep walking this path, you will have a joy in your heart that you did not think you would ever experience. Whether it is the contrast with the prior denial or we are blessed with the unique ability to create it, it is a joy that is the gift of our nature.

This is what I come back to every time. This is what I hold on to when I am struggling. This is what I intend to have define the rest of my life. I do not need to meet some antiquated and arbitrary social standard for what I should look like, for how I should behave, and frankly, neither should anybody reading this. Cis or trans, you do not deserve to live bound by the bars of a prison. You deserve to know what you are supposed to be, and to pursue it wholeheartedly.

If you already know who and what that is, then I hope very much that you are able to find your path to becoming it. If you don't yet know, and especially if the feelings I described of being trapped in a performance you don't want to be a part of resonate with you, I hope that you come to understand what it is you want to be as soon as possible. It came to me later in life than I ever expected, so it may surprise you when it happens.

And finally, to those of you who are so utterly unconfident in what you are that you need to build the whole world into a prison just so that you can feel secure in the structure of its bars, I pity you. The potential is within you, as it is within everybody, to become something unique and extraordinary. Not in the sense of wealth or fame; those don't make you special. There are some spectacularly uninspiring people out there with both of those. But you could be someone who lives how they want to live, not forever defining yourself by comparison to those around you or by your ability to conform to social expectations. You can grow as freely as a flower, irrepressible and driven by your nature to blossom into beauty and complexity and the way you were meant to be.

Flowers cannot grow shut inside a box, they suffer from being crowded by walls and concrete. But they also always strive to reach the clear air and bright sky. We will not stop reaching for that. We will not stop trying to become who we are supposed to be, and any impediment you try to put in our way is limiting yourself and everyone else, too.

Don't you want to be more than that?
I already am.

Ceridwen

Freedom

The world at present, can feel absolute madness. All down to ignorance and prejudice. There are feelings of anger, and a need to be listened to.

Respect should be for all from backgrounds, regardless of religion, identity, sexual orientation, and disabilities. We should all have equality of rights.

We all rise again.
Smile, be happy, think positive.

Julie

Freedom

If you love someone, then set them free.
Do not coerce or try to control me.
I'm not an appendage at the end of your arm.
The way you're behaving is causing me harm.
There's got to be another way, so please cut me some slack.
This isn't about my behaviour but just what you lack.
Insecurity and control sadly go hand in hand.
It's a joke when you ask me to wear a wedding band.
Go work on yourself, give your head a good talking to.
Come back and see me when all of that is through.
Me, I'm moving on to pastures green and new.
No more limitations keeping me in curfew.
I am me, and I am free, and can never be bound.
Inside me is the kingdom you haven't yet found.
Take a moment to reflect why always you've failed.
You've tried to control, your partners you've jailed.
Another way lies waiting if you'd turn around.
Go inside and discover what I have long found.

Terry

Give and you Shall Receive

To give is to receive. You get what you put in. Being nice and friendly to people leads to them being nice and friendly to you. Give gifts to people on occasions, and they will give gifts back to you.

Helping people when they are in need will lead to them helping you when you are in need. This type of reciprocal relationship is echoed throughout humankind and the animal kingdom. It allows for symbiosis, where all can live in harmony and cooperate with each other.

Give and you shall receive.

James

Going Home

Going home to Redcar, on an aging train.
Passing new lambs born, in sunshine, wind, and rain.
Horses gently grazing, dappled mare with foal.
Then a lady feeds them healthy food in a bowl.
Visit every station, then I hear a song.
Another town, another train, it's Abba, sing along!
It's a route I know well, this landscape I so love.
Going home means everything, a blessing from above.

Alison

Growth

Maya Angelou said, 'I rise.' I often felt like life was burying me, down and down, deeper. Restraining me, my creativity, my soul. Now I know I was a seed growing and pushing up towards the light. Breaking through — using the rainfall to learn more and nourish myself.

It felt so dark for so long, I never thought I would break through the layers of soil. At times, it felt there was someone piling more soil on top of me, but I used the manure to grow. They thought that more manure would keep me down. However, it nourished and replenished my nutrients, and I grew every time.

Now, I am a sunflower. I stand tall and proud, showing my beautiful face to the light, leaning towards it for warmth. My stem is no longer thin and fragile. I can sustain myself. I know as I blossom, I will scatter my seeds to help build growth in others. Never-ending, always pushing up to the light.

Rae

Happiness

Happiness is a key of coke.
Happiness is a funny joke.
Happiness is when the family get together.
You can be happy in any kind of weather.
Happiness is looking back with a smile.
Happiness is sticking around for a while.
Happiness is cuddles with the pooch.
Happiness is going for a mooch.
Happiness is bearing no grudge.
Happiness does not judge.
Happiness likes bubbles in its bath.
Happiness is always up for a laugh.
Happiness is growing old.
Happiness doesn't have to fit the mould.
Happiness is making a house a home.
Well, I'm pretty happy, all on my own.

Evie Rose

Hart Gables

My name is Chris and my pronouns are they/them. I have been coming to Hart Gables for five years. The first time I came, was to the Cloud 9 group at the Live Well Centre, then later, we were at the St Mary's Centre. I am happy that Sarah at Steps let me know about the group.

I have lots of happy memories of Hart Gables. The St Mary's Centre was a very special building. It was in the centre of Middlesbrough and Eileen was so kind to us all. I also enjoy doing physical exercise at the Shape and Play sports sessions at Queen's Campus. Some of my happiest memories with Hart Gables are of the Roseberry Topping walks. We do these every year for International Day Against Homophobia, Transphobia, and Biphobia.

I like to wear alternative clothing, gothic fashion and rainbow-coloured. Sometimes, people in society judge me and people who are different, but Hart Gables has always accepted me.

Chris

Hart Gables

Happy

Appreciative of the group

Respectful

Trusting

Great

Associate together

Believe and beautiful

Life, love, liberty

Empathy

Support

Mim, Laye, Olayinka, Gwladys, Imade, Josie

Hart Gables

I first found out about Hart Gables by looking online. I saw Andrew one-to-one; he was helpful, friendly, welcoming, and people who come to the group understand how life can be difficult.

When I leave Hart Gables each week, I feel happier and it helps me to get through each week of difficultness. The group has made my life happier.

Shojib

Help

I knew I had to get away from my current relationship. It never got better, despite him telling me it would and that his abuse towards me was because he was stressed, tired, or because it was my fault. When you are told things like this over and over by someone you love, you believe it. Perhaps it was me — I was always told I was 'no angel' as a child and young adult, so it could have been me who was the problem. He'd tell me I was lucky to have him; that no one else would want me. That I was ugly and useless and stupid and a nag.

It didn't start out like that, with him calling me names, putting me down, hitting me, and spending all the money. I hoped, willed it to return to how it had been at the start of our relationship. Willed him to return to the man I fell in love with. But it never did. He never returned again. He was gone. The good in him died as the bad grew stronger. And along with his growth, I shrunk.

Until one day, I reached out for help and spoke to someone at the 25K Community Centre. They helped me get some specialist support from the refuge and I ended up getting a bed there. I was terrified, but he only threatened me a few times, then left me alone.

I started again. Not just the house, but working through my own issues, with the help and support of services for my mental health. People cared. I was worthy of help, something he made me think I never was. That everything was my fault. I've learnt it wasn't my fault and the support in Redcar helped me realise I can start again. I can be happy and I deserve it.

B

Holy Saturday

I'm waiting for the daffodils,
I transplanted from your old garden.
Hoping over cuttings,
sticking out of rain swollen pots in the back yard.
All there is, is silence.
I'm listening for your voice,
in a dream, in a vision.
I'm searching for a place,
where I might feel your velvet presence.
I'm looking for a sign in the moon rising,
in a specially bright star.
To help me cope with the hollow.
The hole inside that just now cradles your silence.

Kathy

Home

Home is where the heart is.
Home is a place where you live.
Home is security, my safe haven.
Home is where family is.
Memories are made at home.
You make a home; decorate it and put your stamp on it.
I have lived in many homes and many places, but never stayed too long.
I am home now and it is mine.
It mirrors my heart and soul.
Home tells a story of who you are.

Craig

Hope

Hope is an old chandelier, blanketed in dust.
Straining to lift my head to look above.
Weighed down by the tap dripping in the corner, reminding me of days past.
The curtains that have hung for years, blocking the light from creeping in, begin to part.
Shafts of light rush through, changing the air, the atmosphere becomes lighter.
I feel a strong sense inside to lift my head, to follow the light.
To see the hope that's been there all along, be it shrouded in dust.
I blink several times, shake my head and slowly open my eyes to focus on the light.
Each breath brings me closer to hope, and away from the darkness.

Rae

Hummingbird

Hummingbird,
spreads the word, of wonder and joy.
As she sings her sweet song, floats by like a breeze,
so effortlessly, like a hum of a wing.
Her eyes, smile, heart, soul, glistening.
She emanates kindness, curiosity that sparkles.
Ladies like this, they're rare but do exist.
I must persist, if you find one, hold tight.
As she brightens the night,
watch her take flight.
This hummingbird can fight.
But she's soft, calm, humble.
Does anything to avoid a rumble.
Try to be like the hummingbird.
Sing your song; let your voice be heard.
Enchanting by nature, that which her love.
My God, she's an angel, sent from above.
Many have fallen and seen dark days.
Angelic beauty, her colours don't fade.
Her story's not done, she's not staying down.
Encouraged by loved ones, removing the frown.
Armed with a tool box, fit for a challenge.
Right time to hike, forage, and scavenge.
Time ticks on, she's built herself strong.
Let me tell you of hummingbird,
oh, so strong and barely heard.
Visiting flowers, here and there,
effortlessly floating on the air.
Resilient, strong, they'll defend their nest.

Oversized fighting spirit, one of the best.
But don't take my word for it, see for yourself.
Alas, dear hummingbird,
I've tried to spread your word.
Her colours back, she starts to shine.
This little lady is just divine.
My aching heart, you helped to rest.
My broken mind, you did your best.
I'm so glad your sparkle is back,
because you're amazing, and that's a fact.

A Soul Saved

I Changed my own Chemistry

The space between those final words in which I clearly set out my boundaries and the possible next chapter seems uncontrollably lengthy. Time smattered with puddles of anxiety, never knowing how deep each puddle will be, until I'm in. The mantra, 'You didn't hurt them, they have chosen to respond this way. They're hurting themselves' swings round and round like an unfortunate merry-go-round with an ominous soundtrack.

I push my feet firmly into the ground, breathing in for four, hold for four, breathe out, hold for four. I changed my own chemistry, from fight or flight to eggshells. A small improvement, yet noticeable. The uncertainty has always flawed me before. However, now, I respond as me, not who they perceive me to be.

I push my feet firmly into the ground. I breathe in for four, hold four, breathe out, and hold for four. I change my own chemistry. I am me. I am the person it wasn't legal to be when I was younger.

I am me. The me I dreamed of, hoped for and fought to be. I am proud of who I am and how I live my life. I know I'm a good person; people feel lighter in my company. I push my feet firmly into the ground. I breathe in for four, hold four, breathe out, and hold for four.

Rae

I will be me

I am quite shy, mainly when I meet new people or go somewhere I haven't been before — until I am happy in my surroundings. School was a nightmare. I was bullied every day because I wouldn't stand up for myself. I would wear the clothes I was told to wear by my mum. Most of the time, they were okay, but sometimes, I hated them. They just weren't me. My teen years were okay as I got to experiment with clothes and fashion. I got my own style and became more confident with my identity.

My first boyfriend slowly started to comment on the way I looked. He would put me down and make me doubt myself, so I lost a little of myself. After that ended, I slowly came back and made new friends. I promised myself I would never be that way again. No one is going to tell me how to dress and act. I just want to be me, it's allowed. I will be me.

Tracy

Imagine

Imagine a place where you believe in you, and all you can and could achieve.
Where you look in the mirror and speak as a friend.
Instead of listening to the voices, a silly mind may send.
You don't stress, overthink, get angry, or vent.
You pause, take time, breath, and compliment.
In all you've done, endured, enquired, sweet victory.
For each step forward, burns away misery.
You just need to reach out, find someone or something to belong too.
Cos there's nothing sweeter in life, than to have someone to sing along too.
Imagine.

A Soul Saved

Jailer

I often think, *who the hell am I?* A wife, a mother, a grand-mother. Yes, that is me, but is it Marie? Some days, I just don't know. I go around trying to please them all and the only one I leave out is myself. Feeling guilty if I don't achieve it.

Me? *What do I want to be?* Confident, kind, adventurous, and free from responsibility. Not all of the time, but definitely some of the time. I need to give myself permission to enjoy life and not just go through the motions.

I look in the mirror and see this woman looking back at me. *Where did I go?* I miss me, the strong, independent, fun me. I wish she would come back. *But who stops me from returning?* My brain. I'm sadly my own jailer. A life made from too many struggles, tragedy, and heartache, but it's time to break free.

Marie

Justice

Justice is a ship that sails the high seas. A ship is a vessel that helps you travel from one point to another. There is no time that the journey of justice may take. We have seen in many cases, where people have waited decades for justice, like the Hillsborough families, and those wrongly convicted.

The ship called *Justice* must take you somewhere, on some journey. This may be a journey of lessons to learn, a journey of affirmation, but always a journey. Any ship will or should take you somewhere.

I remember someone saying, 'If the ship you are on isn't taking you somewhere, then abandon ship.'

Rae

Light After Dark

In life, you often find the light when you think it's just darkness. My darkness was ongoing. Little did I know how close the light was. My light has come in the form of an amazing person, who until recently, had no idea how dark it had been getting. Unlikely bonds made us closer. Light from a distance makes you remember we are all someone's light, even when we are in darkness and we can all find the light we need. sometimes, when we stop looking for it — light is there.
Zoe

In my life, I have seen much darkness. But nature is balance. Life can't always be bright. A plant needs light as well as darkness to thrive. All things need the sun and the rain, just like the night darkness heightens your senses. I've found the most brilliant and beautiful soils have been forged through darkness. Their light has to shine so brightly to break through it.

Darkness is considered a threat. The terror it instils is just like the fear of death. Yet. The greatest peace you ever feel is a room death has visited to bring an end to suffering. You can't have rebirth without death. Loss makes us see our blessings. You would not see the splendour in light, without the contrast of darkness. It would be dull and lifeless. Balance is needed in all.
Andrea

I am inspired by the anglerfish, who swam to the surface of
the sea from the deep darkness it had been in all its life.
Reaching towards the light, before it took its final breath.

It reminded me that even the smallest of creatures can have a huge impact on the world.

I do believe, we as individuals are guided by our own light, as the anglerfish is, and can have an impact on this world, for good or ill. I choose to look to the light, to follow my internal gut instincts as I move through this world. I will continue to follow the inspiration of the beautiful anglerfish in my life. This, I know, will continue to guide me through the deepest, darkest, most challenging times in my life. Be an anglerfish.
Rae

You are in the dark when you have some issues going on in your life and have no one to help you out. There is always light at the end of the tunnel of everything in life. Everyone in the world has had their own darkest time, but everything is on how you handle your storm and darkness.

I pray for everyone who may have dark days and that these never take over their light in life. I always use my singing and dancing to overcome my darkest times.
Diana

Mental health, depression and anxiety, I have been in darkness. But there is light. It may not be today, it may not be tomorrow, but the light will prevail. Out of darkness, we walk. Darkness is not forever. It is temporary and light always wins.
Craig

Seeing the light after darkness lifts me out of my depressive state from the long, dark days. So, try to enjoy every moment, live for the day, here and now. All things bright and beautiful!
Julie

Light after darkness can mean many things. Like going experiencing anxiety and stress and coming through it. To me, it means I became a champion through this battle; as I suffer from anxiety and depression. It can be stressful at times, but I deal with it and get out of the dark into the light.
Sam

Hitting fifty years old was a bit of a blow to me. People told me, 'That's it now, once you're in your fifties, it all goes downhill'. Well, everything well and truly changed. After my fiftieth birthday, my dad passed away and it broke me. My mood changed, I was crying and snapping at everyone. My relationship ended and for about six months, I was in a dark place. I wanted to be like I used to be: happy, friendly, enjoying a laugh with my friends.

But during this time, I hated everything and everyone. I just wanted to lock myself away from the world. I would get home from work and lock the door, and I hardly spoke to anyone. However, seeing my grandkids made me better but when they left after a visit, it was just me again. Doctors told me it was depression. I had never experienced it before and I didn't want to rely on tablets.

So, I had a good cry and talked to myself; I even talked to my dad. After that day, I got out of bed and went for a walk. During my walks, I met Paul, my now boyfriend and he has been my light. He is amazing and understands me, just gets me. In a few months, we are going to get engaged and we have a bright future.
Tracy

Light After Dark

When we are lost in the night, and afraid to go on.
When we have given up the fight and can't find anyone to call upon.
When it all feels so bleak, and there's nothing inside,
hold on my friend, for the turn of the tide.
I have been there too; I've frequented that place,
I know what it's like to have a sad face.
But faith is the song of the bird before the dawn breaks,
holding out your hand, is all that it takes.
Reach out for me, I'm right by your side,
in me, my friend, you can surely confide.
There is light after dark, night turns to day,
the seasons do change; despair turns to flay.
Be humble and trust and call out my name,
and then you will find that you were never to blame.
Your day is coming, when you'll shine like the sun,
you'll rediscover your life can be such fun.
Light after dark, day after night,
dig deep my good friend, don't give up the fight.

Terry

Long Sentence

Long sentences are being increasingly handed to prisoners as politicians attempt to reduce crime and reoffending with the belief that long sentences give offenders more time to reflect on their crimes and to rehabilitate their behaviours while protecting the community from crime with the lengthy sentences acting as a deterrent to other criminals and acting as an adequate punishment of their offences to both the offenders and victim's lives however long sentences often lead to prisoners becoming institutionalised and reliant on prison regimes and structures with little or no active rehabilitation offered due to the lack of funding for behavioural courses to reduce offending and criminal behaviours with the courses that are offered only being made available at the end of sentences this leaves inmates often unable to adapt to returning into the community due to the length of time that the long sentences have kept them out of the community this leads to prisoners developing mental health problems and substance misuse problems as the vulnerable prisoners struggle to cope and comprehend the unnatural and often dangerous environments in which they must live and serve lengthy sentences so to adapt and cope with the ever-changing world that they are to re-enter the damaged prisoners often have to rehabilitate and prepare themselves to re-enter a society of self-reliance and opportunity as they leave a restricted society that they have existed in for significant length of time under the repetition of the prison regime and restricted freedoms where the prisoners have either been the victims or perpetrators of crime whilst in prison as a lack of meaningful activities and structures worsened by the length of sentence and lazy or corrupt or inexperienced staff failing to control the environment which often leads to anarchical behaviour and attitudes as some prisoners become ruthlessly manipulated and take advantage of those around them by acting alone or in gangs who inflict violence and intimidate to take advantage of others in an endless cycle as they fight to survive or thrive in the ruthlessly dysfunctional environment and society which is often left leaderless and controlled by those hired by the government to provide authority who are often under trained or who worsen the environment by encouraging violence or in providing the drugs which have flooded the prison wings feeding the anarchical beast of lawlessness within the UK prison state which is filled to maximum capacity worsened by underfunding and increasing amounts of lengthy sentences being handed by the courts or refused paroles due to the lack of rehabilitation or the revolving door of licence recalls a vulnerable and unadapted prisoners by probation taking them from the streets to the world where they are not helped to walk and return to a world filled with some of the country's most dangerous individuals and some formerly decent members of society who have broken the law having made poor decisions or judgments and now must navigate their unnatural world suffering complex issues of poor mental health and trauma which often leads to self-harm and suicide as a method to cope with being forced into an environment which is infamous for acts of violence and manipulation through tactics of intimidation by prisoners and prison officers who are employed to provide safety and offer assistance to prisoners as they exist in their long sentences and prepare for their eventual release into society which will require adaptation to a completely different lifestyle from which they have grown used to knowing to having to learn self-reliance in finding work and providing for themselves in order to become a functional and productive member of society having been reliant on the prison service for a significant length of time which has provided their essential needs and routines of a fairly predictable prison regime where prisoners are locked away behind doors with lock and key and have adapted for many years while living aimlessly and without meaning but are expected to make sense of a long sentence and reintegrate with minimal support back into a functional and ever-changing society.

So, if this long sentence didn't make sense to you, imagine being a prisoner.

Anthony

Lost and Found

Sometimes you don't realise you're lost until you are found.
Lost.
Like an umbrella left on a train — handed in, registered.
Lost.
That was me, travelling around.
Lost.
Until I was found, helped, supported.
And my life changed, improved.
My happiness and mood, more positive.
Purpose.
A future.
Goals.
A light.
I was found.

Matthew

Make a Person Welcome

It is the most wonderful feeling to be made welcome. It can be in someone's home, at an event, at an appointment, or while visiting hospital. Some random event that a person attends can be the place that opens a welcoming door. That one person that you just recently met, smiling, reserving a seat for you.

'Would you like a cup of tea?'

And to top that, being interested in your work. It is also important to welcome visitors if you are the host or if people are calling at your home. That kind deed can be so appreciated and it does feel good knowing you have made that person's day!

Make a person welcome.
It can really make their day.
A friendly atmosphere and such a lot to say.
Talking of their country, their home they love to live.
Singing all together, with such a lot to give.
May this welcome feeling, spread around our earth.
It is something we can feel, from when we are given birth.

Alison

Mental Health and Me

It's good to be sad sometimes, to clear my mind of any issues that are happening in my life. Listening to music can sometimes make me feel sad. 'All by Myself' by Celine Dion never fails to bring me to tears.

At the time the song came out, I had come out of a long-term relationship with my son's dad. I thought I was by myself, not realising that I wasn't by myself at all, and I'm still not. I have my son and a network of family and friends. I still feel sad when I hear this song, even though it was years ago and I have moved on with my life.

I've been through bouts of depression in my life and a breakdown, blaming myself for things that have happened in my life. I've had suicidal thoughts and taken an overdose. What got me through my struggles was the image of my son and the realisation of what would happen to him if I succeeded in ending my life.

Support through counselling and therapy, experts and my GP has helped me tremendously. I have learnt to deal with issues that trigger my sadness. Also, mediation, soft music, talking, and support groups help and are very valuable to me, and it's free to access these services.

I feel proud of myself for what I have achieved over the years, through thick and thin. So, I thank my family, my son, Carer's Together, North East Opera, and Terry.

Julie

Moonlight

Moonlight was pouring its light in your eyes.
I was watching, my eyes gazed on the mirror, on your pupils.
Looking for stroke love, stroke harvest.
Inside your eyes, was a forest after a rainy day.
Dew in your eyes, wetting your eye's lashes.
Under the rain, my track was gone since your hands disappeared.
The night held a full moon.
Your face was behind the dim shadow.
I am lost looking for your home direction.
I left your address on my mirror.
No harvest, even though it is raining here without your love.
Moon is full but not pouring light in my eyes.
Moor inside your eyes, I can't see how can I survive without you.
I lost your home; your eyes, my heart harvest in dusk.

Zainab

Mum's Advice

My mum always gave good advice. Sometimes it was needed, and sometimes I thought to myself, *what the hell did she know?* But often enough, I would still go to her and get some much-needed advice.

Having three children and being on my own was tough. Days were never the same. Some days were okay, but some days were like hell. The kids would be playing up, the house would be a mess. Plus, I would be skint. But somehow, my mum always knew when I needed her and she would ring me or she would turn up on the doorstep.

We would sit with a cuppa or she would play with the kids. Most of the time, she would get them all to clean their rooms. Also, she would make a meal out of things I had in the cupboard. Things that I wouldn't use for a meal; it was like magic.

Now I find myself doing the same things for my own daughter, helping her like my mum did me. Giving her more or less the same advice my mum did for me. And sometimes I hear myself as if I were my mum giving the advice. Spooky!

I say to my daughter, 'You will get days like this when nothing is going right, but the next is a new day and it's okay to start over.'

Tracy

My Colourful Garden

Wallflowers in my garden,
have bloomed in every shade.
Bright as all the solar lights,
just as the daylight fades.
Yellow, reds, and orange,
what blessings nature brings.
And it seems whatever time,
the garden songbird sings.
Sometimes, this is solo,
or birdsong all together.
Thanks for my colourful garden,
so much grows in different weather.

Alison

My Community

It was the late 70s, early 80s when I first felt the sharp, cold sword of judgement. At the age of four or five, I knew that certain clothes and hairstyles made me feel physically ill. However, the parental judgement leant heavily and my needs seemed to be unheard or unwanted.

Many rows later, particularly on a Sunday morning when apparently, it was the done thing to 'look like a lady in church', I couldn't cope anymore. I walked away with my baseball cap and skin-fade haircut from the barbers. My soul couldn't take the sharp, cold sword of judgement anymore.

A day hasn't gone by from then until 2022, when I wasn't stared at in the streets, heckled at, or told I was in the wrong toilets. Or even worse, physically or verbally assaulted by judgemental people. In 2022, I moved to Seaton Carew in Hartlepool. From day one, deep in the coldness of a January day, I was welcomed. I was treated with respect and, at times, cared for and loved.

For the first year, it felt odd not to be on edge, always still waiting for that judgement. It's taken some time, but now I can say I haven't experienced hate crime or negative judgement here in those years. Life is lighter, fresher, calmer. I've found my people, my community. I am safe here, physically and emotionally and I can say that I will never take this for granted.

Rae

My Great Folk

It was not a joke, a tornado of culture and song.
We filled the main hall, young, old, small, and tall.
From all walks of life, people came along.
They clapped to the beat with this musical treat.
The talent on stage it uncurled.
To showcase their stories in music and sound,
of folk from all over the world.
The violin skipping, the drums strong and loud,
the piano sweet talking away to the crowd.
Diversity bounced from all parts of the world,
with each song, yet another layer uncurled.
A ballerina elegantly danced the stage floor,
to the voice of an opera star, moved us to the core.
A collaboration of musical history,
that kept them spellbound like ancient history.
Middlesbrough has determination, guts, and foundations.
My great folk, we spoke out to the nations.

Mel

My Home

Home, my home. When shall I see my home? When shall I see my native land? I will never forget my home. My home is a place where I have peace and love. Where I dance, at home. Where I sing, at home. And praised worship.

I feel like I am on the moon whenever I am home, with the people that matter to me and in my community. I look like the queen I am, in the home, with my people.

Do you know the difference between home and house? Home is quiet and peaceful. Whilst house is noisy always. I feel peace when I'm at home rather than in my house. When I look at my home, I am happy. When I look at my home, I smile because that's where my happiness comes from.

Now that people are put in indefinite detention, when you think of home, you will feel the pain of when will my voice come out from my home? For people to know what I have been through when I was far away from home.

Home is home. Anywhere you go, don't forget home.

Diana

My Story

When I started going to Hart Gables in 2009, I had no one. I'd lived in Hartlepool all my life, and my family had been there for me, until I came out as transgender, and they wouldn't be around me anymore. My mum, my brother, my sister, my niece — all of them shut the door on me. But it wasn't a choice for me; it's the person I am.

I've been in some dark places. Trying to go out and about in Hartlepool, after coming out as trans, it just wasn't good. One time, I went into town and came back with two black eyes, a broken nose, and a fat lip. It affects your mental health. At one point, I made a suicide attempt. No one can go through all that on their own. Hart Gables was there for me. For fifteen years, they've been a safe and supportive place for me. I'd lost my family, but I was accepted as part of the LGBTQ+ family.

Through Hart Gables, I've been able to do and see things I never would have otherwise. I've gone to study sea life at a laboratory with Newcastle University, and gone to Pride events that I never would have been able to afford or had the confidence to go to myself. I've been involved in so much. I go regularly to groups and get one-to-one support, but I've also been a Forum Champion for trans women, talking to professionals in the area about the issues we face.

I've given speeches about hate crime to Cleveland Police, helping them to understand the impact of hate crime on an emotional level and on mental health. I've done guest talks at events for International Day Against Homophobia, Transphobia, and Biphobia. I've helped with business planning and writing the charity's strategies. I've offered friendship and support to newer members at the Hart Gables groups, using my experience to help other people feel welcome and safe.

I had my surgery, about four years ago. Hart Gables supported me all the way through this, on the phone to me while I was in hospital. As I got more confidence, I got more friends. I have a wider circle of friends in Middlesbrough now who I can also rely on. My friend Amanda and her partner have been amazing.

After my surgery, I felt ready to look for a job, after being on jobseekers and then universal credit since I left school. I've held down a job now for years, and I've recently been successful in an interview for a second job. I hope to be off Universal Credit altogether eventually. I still need travel expenses to groups, though and still struggle sometimes with money to buy food. Hart Gables helps with this.

After I got forced out of Hartlepool because of hate, I came to Middlesbrough with two black bags of clothes and nothing else. I really believe that if it wasn't for Hart Gables, I'd be dead. Everyone needs people in their corner. Hart Gables are in mine.

Julie Ann

Nature's Night Light

Nature's night light is shining down,
on where it once was dark.
Outlining all the shapes of trees,
the shadows, twigs, and bark.
Though I've added my own beam,
that spans and glows around.
It's nature's night light that will guide,
illuminate the land.
As people work the twilight hours,
glad when the night shifts over.
It's nature's night light that brings peace,
a spotlight on the clover.
So, feeling healed from the bright moon,
my thanks, I'd like to give.
For helping all creation to,
expand, grow strong, and live.

Angela

Never Leave our Love

All butterflies for you.
I keep the roses to remember you.
Even when I miss you,
they wound my fingers with their thorns.
Next sunrise, I'll be waiting for spring with you.
Come across my doubts to make sure you never lose my love.
Let's never say goodbye to butterflies.

Zainab

New Beginnings

I have had a few fresh starts in life, new chapters. But moving back to Hartlepool, home to my spirit family, my true family, is a new book in my life. I have started afresh. Thrown out the old volumes, only keeping pages that enrich my life. My family keeps growing. Lovely, bright souls appearing in my world, like spring flowers. I've finally sprung. With new blooms, come new opportunities.
Andrea

Starting over from a bad day, seeing the sunrise on a morning and hearing the birds singing, always helps me prepare for the day ahead. Whatever the day will bring, I'm thankful for the little things. Take time to notice, smell the flowers, and smile.
Tracy

New beginnings are everywhere, not just in nature. We are all born and we all begin. New beginnings can be sad and painful. Loss of someone or something. Like the Celtic circle of life, everything begins again but I think are we being given an opportunity to do things better next time around? Have we spread love this time and not hatred and discontent?
Cecilia

It's a new day, so it's your brains time to do its thing. But what happens when it's exhausted? Today, I choose not to give in. Tomorrow is another day, a new day and a new beginning. And we are all entitled to have as many new beginnings as we need.
Marie

Every day is a new beginning. The past has gone, the future a mystery. In this present moment, we received the gift of new life. Just as every new day is a new beginning for me, it is for every living soul, no matter how horrible their yesterday may have been.

Terry

Every day, there's something new,
announcing hope, a baby too!
In the street, spring in the air,
a baby in a blue pushchair.
Doting parents, looks of love,
blessings come from up above.
Children smile, giggle, so happy,
they're not long in their nappy.
Paint some pictures, play in sand,
run together hand in hand.
We have proved, there is no end.
New beginnings, blessings send.

Alison

No Reason

No reason that I can think of, for the tears that sprang unhid-
den.
Triggered by something in the news.
Or a flitting thought, memory, chemical blip, or mood swing.
No reason but once started, the tears brought more tears.
More tears, until I wept myself dry.
Bleak, empty eyes, and heart and soul.
Yet, I'm still here.
The moment passed, undoubtedly to reoccur sometime.
And I'm still here.

Alan

No Shame

Don't tell me what to think, a facade to be kind.
Spew words in my ears, try to influence my mind.
Opinions on my choices of this and that.
Rolling of the eyes, judgement sat.
For making a choice, that's only mine to make.
No confirming, no following, playing a high stake.
Just as your life is yours, as is the path that you walk.
Others travel another route, talk a different talk.
Live and let live, no shunning, no shame.
Life would be without colour if we were all the same.

Anon

Number One

Whatever I give, I give to myself. Yes, the world does revolve around me. The reason I'm so important is that for me to receive, I have to be number one. I am the bee's knees. I am the head of 'Kool and the Gang'. I am safe in my sovereign power. Safe upon my royal seat.

But guess what? I neither look up to anyone nor down to anyone. So, the reason I am number one and put myself first is because there is no number two, number three, or number four. No one above and no one below. We are all one.

I am the king and queen. I reign. Like the many raindrops that are part of the ocean, which is where they come from and journey back to, we are all part of the ocean of life: an ocean of love. As the raindrops take their journey back to their source, they do so with ease and flow, choosing the path of least resistance. So ultimately, I'm neither a giver or a receiver.

Go up into space and tell me which direction is above and which direction is below?

Glen

Ode to Neo

NEO, such a unique group,
that meets each week and sing in a loop.
It's more than just singing, a thought we can share.
You don't have to sign, just sit in that chair.
And listen to the gift which brings us together,
from a bellowing sound or soft like a feather.
We carry sunshine, blue skies and rain,
hardship, sadness, laughter, and pain.
But whatever our circumstances and mood,
singing gives us our musical food.
David doesn't need a microphone,
especially with that rumbling baritone!
His passion for voice is a gift from above,
filling the air with feeling and love.
Emily, full of beauty, fun, and flair,
but sing it wrong and you'll get that stare!
The piano notes flow like a rippling stream,
and percussion tones from the tambourine.
We guarantee to touch your heart.
We'll have you watching right from the start.
And you'll always remember who we are,
not any old opera: NEO North East Opera.

Mel

One Life

We are human.
We are born and we die.
It is what you do in between that matters.
Live, and enjoy your life!
Don't let things get you down.
Stand tall and strong.
There will be dark times.
But light will overcome darkness.
Have faith and believe.
We have one life — make the most of it!

Craig

Our Middlesbrough

'Yer jokin', aren't ya?' said Gazbo. 'We've just been voted the worst place to live in Britain.'

'Well, ya know what?' his mate, Dunny, replied, 'I'm proud to be called a Smoggie!'

And yes, I am! People from outside the area can label Teesside as a dump; polluted with the legacy of its heavy industrial past. Or 'The Werks', as they're known locally. But I am proud to be born and bred in South Bank, amidst a very Irish Catholic, solidly working-class, salt-of-the-earth community.

Yes, there's pollution still, but in comparison to years ago, we've really cleaned up our act. Yes, sadly, there are high levels of unemployment and poverty in certain areas and I'm not going to deny that. But let's look beyond, to our rolling hills, to Eston Nab, to Roseberry Topping, and to our miles of golden beaches. We've got the North Yorkshire Moors on our doorstep and the mighty Boro down by the riverside. And our steel helped build the world, the railways, the bridges. Our men grafted long hours to dig out the iron ore from the deep, dark, and dangerous underground — to be smelted and forged into steel. Yes, truly, we are men and women of iron!

'Boro's just a dump' is a myth, a fairytale. The Boro I know is an honest town with no pretension and its people are solid and reliable, honest as the day is long. The salt of the earth to be sure anawl, anawl! Give me Teesside over snobby land wherever, all day long! I'm proud to be a Smoggie and that will be my song! Up the Boro!

Terry

Middlesbrough to me, is an anglerfish. It swims in the darkest of places due to its lack of employment and decline of its historical industries. It's been pushed down deep into the darkness by austerity, swimming often along with no external light to sustain it. However, its spirit and heart shine brightly all over through other people and their kindness and generosity.

Middlesbrough is the anglerfish of the sea. A bit scary to look at, at first, but it carries its own light. It has inner strength to continue through the challenges of the darkness, using its own light. The spirit of the people — Middlesbrough will strive forward through the light of kindness of its people.
Rae

There are lots of things amazing about Middlesbrough, such as Middlesbrough winning and being promoted to Premiership. Beautiful views, steelworks, migration, multi-cultural society, people wanting to help each other. Our historic buildings, universities and colleges. Art galleries, museums, the Transporter Bridge, Stewart Park, the birthplace of Captain Cook.
Craig

Middlesbrough has such a history as a place and it's my history. I remember walking over the Transporter Bridge as a child with my father and two brothers. The traditional brass bands that played Christmas songs — the Salvation Army with their annual Christmas carols in the hospital. I remember this happening when I had my son and it was lovely to hear them sing. Each year, the Boro football players visit our local hospital to give poorly children Christmas gifts. It brings joy to the children's faces as they see their favourite Boro players!

There is a Christmas light switch on for local buildings and the Transporter Bridge and Newport Bridge are lit up all night. Christmas markets offer food: lots of cakes and not forgetting the traditional mulled wine. I'm proud to be a Smoggie!
Julie

Middlesbrough was a place I had never heard of until the day I came here. My first day in Middlesbrough was like hell to me and I thought I couldn't do anything here because I didn't know anyone around here. But on that very day, something strange happened to me that changed my thinking and perspective.

During my wallowing in pain, I met some people who gave me the support I thought I could never get. Support on how to adapt to my new way of living and talked about the people I would meet on my way and how to cope with my pains and sorrows.

In the beginning, I thought it's not going to be easy. But with the spirit of hope I got from the people I met, it gave me and continues to give me big motivation that I will be fine and just to keep going. Today, I thank God and the people around me who gave me the strength to overcome my fear of the unknown.
Diana

People Care

When services work together, they can achieve more. Most people who work at charities and such places do care. Many have been there themselves, worn the t-shirt, and they know what they are talking about. They can give advice, guidance, and be a light in the dark. That first step is always the hardest. Walking into somewhere new and asking and answering questions.

If it's done in the right way, with kindness, compassion, and patience, it can save someone's life. The services in Middlesbrough have saved my life, and I will forever be grateful and proud of where I come from, where I live.

In the future, the near future at that, I will volunteer and hopefully be a trusted person who many people can talk to. Like the workers I have had.

Aaron

Positive Impact

Told to legally lie on official papers, lie at the doctors, on my passport, even my birth certificate.
My deed poll proves, at least in name, I am legal.
You see, my sex is not my gender.
I'm non-binary, which means that I don't feel male or female.
I want to be me. Is that not allowed? Not in this country.
So, I'm not legal or illegal, not seen, not believed, or heard.
Part of who I am is invisible.
Yet so very visible to those who know and love me.
Strange really, even growing up, it was not lawful for me to be a parent as I wished.
Illegal to foster and adopt. So really, I've not been allowed to be me in some way, forever.
However, I know this invisible, illegal human makes waves in this world.
And others like me make a positive impact on this world — and that really matters.

Rae

Power to Change

To give is to receive; there is no reprieve.
In life, if you do not give, a lonely life you'll lead.
Everyone has needs.
How are they fulfilled?
By some kind heart giving.
It's just like sowing a seed.
The person who receives might then do just the same.
So, one small act of giving has the power to change the world.
More hope, more faith in people, like a necklace grown from one small pearl.

Cecilia

Put it on the Slate

I was six years old. It was Saturday and I was hungry, again. A school day would have been better. At least I had a piece of bread and margarine shoved into my hand with some sugar on it, as I passed through the front door. And now and then, a castor oil capsule in winter, which repeated on me all morning. My old dad, who was in his fifties, hadn't a clue. It seemed like Mum was never around. I put my black patent leather shoes on. Lovely and shiny, but fading now, because I couldn't see my face in them anymore. I set off, not knowing where I was going and no one in the house to tell where I was going.

I only knew I had a threepenny piece in my pocket to go to the Marly — the Marlborough cinema — that afternoon. It was raining quite heavily; freezing, and I had no coat. Around the corner, I came to the sweet shop, Garnetts. It sold everything, not just sweets but groceries and health remedies too.

On looking in the window, I saw the biggest glass container of salted peanuts I'd ever seen! And I was so, so, so hungry! I looked at the lady serving. *She's the one who likes my mother and always chats to her. I bet she'll like me as well. Perhaps enough to give me some of those peanuts. She never wanted any money from Mum, either. Not one coin passed between the two adults. Strange that,* I thought.

All I heard was my mother say, 'Put it on the slate.'

'Okay, Maggie,' was the reply.

So, I went in and brazenly asked for some salted peanuts.

'Salted peanuts. How many do you want?'

Well, then I had to think on my feet, because the only measurement I knew was a pound. 'A pound of this and a pound of that,' I had heard my mother say.

So, I said, 'A pound.'

'A pound?' she replied. 'Are you sure?'

'Yes,' I said.

'Has your mother asked for these?'

'Yes,' I said.

So, she weighed them out and told me the price. With my heart thumping in my chest, I grabbed the nuts and shouted back at her as I went through the door, 'Put it on the slate!'

Just like my mother did. Before she could answer, I was gone into the alleyway, tearing open the bag and stuffing myself with salted peanuts. At first, they were lovely, but then I started to fee thirsty and the rain became the thing I most wanted. I put my head back to catch raindrops in my mouth. Eventually, I threw the bag away. *Serves me right,* I thought.

A few days later, I came in from school and headed for the kitchen to find something to eat, but there was rarely anything. Many parents in those days relied on free school meals at lunchtime to feed their children. Suddenly, I heard my mother calling me from the front room. *How odd*, I thought, *she's never in!* I entered the room.

She kept saying, 'Come closer, come closer.'

What was I supposed to see? She was holding a long, thin piece of white paper in her hand at arm's length. She looked calm enough but there was something about her eyes I didn't like — a bit like a snake that's about to pounce on its prey.

'Come closer,' she said.

So, I did and then I saw the word on the paper: PEANUTS. It was a till receipt from the shop and my arm was being clasped in a vice-like grip and I had suddenly turned into a rag doll that could scream.

Cecilia

RC

This one's not about the dark, the light, or my misery.
This is a shout to the thanks, to the choice that's been put in front of me.
It's time to stop crying in shame.
The anger with pain. All of the rage.
Pick up a pen, turn a new leaf; start a new page.
It all starts with a man and a flower.
They help lost souls, guide them to a higher power.
A place filled with love and affection.
People trying to make a connection.
Cos we're all trying to kill an infection; get you staring at your reflection.
Looking at what's deep inside,
all you have to do is open your mind.
Let the team help you explore, past and history.
Trust me, someone's been there before.
I confess, whatever you've been through,
I protest, that the team has got you.
For me, it was Poppy and Peter, bless the gods, I'm so glad I got to meet ya.
I could take every day, to shower you with praise,
But you'd just cheekily smile, nod, tell me to go away,
as you say, 'This is just what we do.'
That's just two, I'll do my best to name some of the other crew.
Before I do, a shoutout to lil hummingbird.
I just think they're beautiful, I'd like to spread the word.
There's Jo, current head of the ship.
Full of wonder and wit, she shoots from the hip.

She leads the team, loud and proud,
impossible problems just can't be found.
I wish I had the time to put everyone's words in rhyme.
There's Mark C, Mark E, Jade, Nick, Miret, and Terry.
Adam, Col, James, Jackie, Em, and Jen.
This list is never ending, why the F did I begin?
Oh yeah, a shoutout to RC, all it's done for me.
Shown me who I can be, if I set out to achieve.
If you just believe, you can build.
Physically, mentally, spiritually, and be the better thee.
If you just choose to be; instead of what is, or what was, or never was.
Become something new, become a better you.

A Soul Saved

Reach Out

Screaming used to echo in my head, continuous, yet it wasn't my voice.
Repeated, like a stuck record. Everyone else, unaware of the noise.
Aggressive, argumentative, abrupt; making me think I was going insane.
Intimidating, irritating, insidious. Never going away.
Hovering, getting louder, taking over.
Silence wasn't really a thing — I couldn't get any respite.
Low mood, depression, despair.
Eventually, I knew, it would get me.
Now I had to stop it, I had to find me again.
Confidence in tatters but still I reached out.
Got help me and now I feel me again.

Mark

Sam's Story

A few years ago, I came to meet a young man — barely twenty years old — sleeping rough under the warm air duct outside of a leisure centre. I sat next to him and struck up a conversation. It was evident he was a troubled soul, struggling with life, and estranged from his family. I explored if he was accessing support, but it became clear that he wasn't ready to trust anyone. So, I did what I could do — and that was to listen to what he had to say.

To protect his anonymity, I will call him 'Sam'. Sam said his father had left the family home for another woman. It had broken Sam's heart; his father was his hero. Not long after, Sam's mam struck up a relationship with another man, who bullied Sam at every opportunity. He missed his dad so much. Sam tolerated the situation as long as he could but found himself staying away from school and got in with the wrong crowd. They introduced him to heroin, aged fifteen, to numb the pain. The first time Sam smoked heroin, he was sick to the core, physically. But mentally and emotionally, he felt safe and he felt peaceful. Heroin promises much and ultimately delivers nothing, and Sam was finding this out the hard way.

How will this story end? Who knows? For now, all I or anyone else can do is sit alongside Sam, listen, and feed him with food and love. Hopefully, soon, Sam will be ready to heal and go on to live his life. He's like so many hurt and broken souls doing their best to find light amidst their personal darkness. Will you be willing enough not to judge a book by the cover and bring some light of hope into someone like Sam's life?

Terry

Seagull

Seagull, never been dormant.
Being an immigrant, I wished to be a bird.
A seagull bird, who lives with the winds, happily, and tend.
Flying from beginning to the end.
Being free, flying as sky ruler.
Governor of clouds, a peace messenger.
I would give each passenger a tulip, hidden in magical power.
I would fly to stop all wars, no matter how far the landmark might be.
Bring them an armistice. Spread light through the dark, dim houses.
I'd drop warmth to the shivering bodies.
In winter, I would drop food and flow for the homeless to stop what they are going through.
If I were a seagull, I'd stop death from taking children's smiles.
I would make everyone's hands kinder than tinder.
I woke up from my dream. I dropped the last pieces of bread to seagulls eating in peace.
Farewell to the next sea tides, vases in peace.

Zainab

Sharing

The world is round, so they say, 'What goes around comes around'.
I live by the saying, 'Treat everyone as you would like to be treated'.

Sadly, not everyone does. It seems big companies only ever consider profit, which usually means the little people suffer. The rich get richer and the poor get poorer. What do multi-millionaires think about spreading the wealth? Why have so much money that you could never spend in your lifetime? It's not just money, it is time, dignity, togetherness, and kindness that make us rich. To make a difference in someone's life, no matter how small it is, is such a good feeling.

I spent quite a few years being a carer, going to people's homes. My role could be making a cuppa or washing and dressing someone. Or to sit and have a chat with them. Maybe I was the only human interaction they would have that day. Then I went to work in a nursing home. Often short-staffed, poorly paid, and with no breaks. That was the downside. But I always kept in mind that the people living there were someone's mam, nana, dad, grandad, uncle, or aunt.

How would I like my family to be looked after? So, no matter how stressful and tiring the day was, I always went home with such a good feeling. Listening to tales of someone's childhood, how they met the love of their life. Wartime stories, all the magic, I could feel. I was making a difference, albeit small and sweet, but it made me feel so good.

Marie

Soulmates

I have spent a lifetime giving to others and very rarely got anything in return. I don't ask for anything, or want, or expect. However, when you find true soulmates — friends who have become family, you get what you give. You never keep score on who did what for who.

It's just even the smallest acts of kindness that really count. Truly equal love in deeds and the heart. I feel such joy in giving, more than to receive, but when it is shared, it's priceless.

Andrea

Standing Together

Together we are stronger to tackle adversity, bigotry, discrimination, and prejudice.
To support each other as community groups and support groups in times of trouble.
To accept people from different backgrounds, religions, sexual orientations, and cultural backgrounds.
To enable everybody to gather together to fight all adversities in life in an appropriate way.
To be listened to.
To respect other people's opinions.
The world would be a better place if we all stand together.

Julie

Straining for Hope

The dark clouds lifted; the air felt lighter. Hope dangled from the ceiling. Like an old chandelier, draped in dusk, it had been there all along, but my head was too heavy to lift.

Today, my shoulders were lower, my stomach did not churn. My breath seemed to come from deeper in my lungs rather than the quick, shallow pants of before. The creak of the door didn't alert my senses. I stood more firmly and raised my head, holding tightly to all my truths.

I've got this.
I am a good person.
I am worth more than I feel.
I've got this.
I am a good person.
I am worth more than I feel right now.

I stood firmly and raised my head, straining for hope. She was there, looking towards me. Holding out her welcoming hands with a knowing smile that said *I'm here, I've got you.*

Rae

Strength in Together

Alone, we feel scared, shy, and uneasy in certain situations. Life has shown us to stay quiet; keep your mouth shut. Don't show your true feelings, hide away from confrontation — just in case you hurt someone or someone hurts you.

As I get older and hear the news, it's telling us about other people getting killed or jailed for crimes. Maybe if they were heard or treated with a bit more kindness, their lives would be different.

When I was younger, I was taught to be kind and respect my elders. I think people have forgotten this. There is more anger in the world now. If one person can show kindness, why can't the rest? Because together, we are stronger.

Tracy

Support

Support is there, if you reach out.
Understanding that you're not alone.
People care; they want to help.
Please don't struggle alone.
Open up and talk.
Rather than feeling there's no hope.
Trust that people care.

Emma

The Inner Struggles and Strength of Just One Person

I know I'm not the only one who has been through the mill but this is my story. All my life, the universe has put me on a rollercoaster since birth to now. But all through my life, I have left my mark on people in one way or another. And after writing this, I hope I have left an even bigger mark long after I've gone. But I want to talk about my early to mid-forties, where my life turned upside down and turned up right again.

So, this is where it started: on the 30th March 2023, my back began to tighten up. I just thought it was to do with my spine playing up, like it does. It happened again the next day. On 1st April, everything seemed to have settled down with my back, so on that day, I started to lift and move several concrete slabs in my back garden and I felt fine. However, on the 2nd April, something was really wrong. I couldn't put my finger on what was going on with me and I rang for an ambulance.

I was admitted to hospital where they told me I had experienced a few heart attacks over that past week. On the 4th of that month, I had a stent put in. Before I had the stent put in, I had to sign some form and the DNR form came up. I refused to sign it and told the medical staff to do what they needed to keep me alive as I still had things to do! However, I didn't know what that was at that point in my life as I've always looked after other people's interests before my own.

If there is one thing I realised, it was that there were no particular symptoms for my heart attacks. So, I would say, if you think there is something wrong, get it checked straight away and don't leave it like I did.

Later that year, on the 17th September 2024, I woke up and

it felt like there was a universe exploding in my head. I struggled on my own for a month to try and workout what was going through my mind, but I could not figure anything out. In the end, I wrote everything down that was going through my head and started to google some of my thoughts. However, I did not self-diagnose, as that is the worst thing to do! Instead, I made a doctor's appointment, where they could diagnose me — that is the right thing to do as self-diagnosis can be dangerous, no matter what your issues are.

When I went to see the doctor, I could not put it into words what was going on with me so I gave the doctor what I had written down. When she read my thoughts, she said she will need to refer me to the gender clinic as she believed I had gender dysphoria.

When I got home, my brother knew there was something wrong with me because I was not myself. I couldn't tell him my thoughts and what had happened at the doctor's. I let him read what I had shown my doctor.

His remarks after reading it was, 'You're still my family.' On that Friday, he had to go away for a bit but in the days before, when he was with me, I couldn't have asked for any more support from one person. He is away now and I have struggled because my close supportive person is not around.

After he had gone, I felt like I was sinking and I didn't know if I had any more mental strength left in me to cope. So, I had to figure out what my next move was going to be and that is when I contacted Hart Gables and they said that there was a support group that afternoon and would I like to go?

Since I have been going to the support group, I have come a long way in a short space of time. It can take years for someone to get where I am. In the space of three to four months on, I now know I have got all the inner strength to fight, no matter what life throws at me.

How I came up with my middle name, Rose, is a nice story. I was 21 years old and I went to an old friend's house. She knew me when I was younger and also knew I use to dress up in female clothing.

She said, 'Let me make you over.'

Me being me, I said, 'Okay then!'

I was over the moon with what she had asked, so she gave me a body suit with suspenders and stockings and a skirt with a rose pattern on it to wear. Then, she did my makeup. After getting dressed and having my makeup applied, she asked me to go with her to pick her children up from school.

That was the first and only time I had went out as a female and it felt so right. Back then, over twenty years ago, I didn't know the term for it like I do now. That's why I chose the middle name Rose, because it feels right — just like it did back then with the rose-patterned skirt I wore.

Since I have come out a trans-female, I have also come out of my shell. I am a lot happier, more outgoing, and I know who I am, and who I could be. I still have bad days, but most of them are good days now. I'm me and I am still in the beginning of my transition from male to female. If there is one thing I could tell you, it is that you are not alone. There are some amazing people out there who will give you the support and advice you need. Don't suffer alone. Speak to someone and never feel ashamed of who you are or who you want to be.

Kelly Rose

The Report

James is a bright student who is always punctual and is always dressed appropriately. He has no problem with the work that is done and may find some of it particularly easy, depending on what topics we are working on. My issues with James arise during class discussions and similar parts of the class.

James will never contribute during these and when calling upon James, he suddenly is very stifled, hesitant, and lacking in eloquence in his speech. This is reflected in his answers, which are simply unsatisfactory at times.

I know that James is bright and I expect more from him. A similar issue arises when working in groups. James does not help the group get through the work; he seems to forget that they are even in a group in the first place. He clearly lets the other group members do most of the work, which I would not expect of James at all, as he does not struggle with the work. Even more than discussion and group work, there are also my issues I have with him with class presentation.

Well, well, let me tell you about that…

James

The Truth Shall Set You Free

One night, whilst in utter despair, I cried out to God for help. Some atheist I was! I couldn't even get that right. Without thinking about it, I fell to my knees, crying and pleading to God for help. Within two minutes, I was in bed, and upon wakening, I had forgotten about that event the night before — which turned out to be something very big in my life.

Over the next six months, my life slowly began to transform. One day, whilst standing outside of a church in Whitby. The plaque on the wall read, *'The truth shall set you free.'*

Whilst reading this, I was filled with an overwhelming sense of peace and complete contentment. After around a minute of wonder and awe, I remembered being on my knees, crying out to God. This was the moment I realised there was no going back; the moment I felt freedom from my trauma.

I never thought I believed in any type of God and still don't believe in certain ideas of what or who God is. For me, God is the universal intelligence, which beats the heart, digests our food, heals the cut on my finger, rotates the earth around the sun, and keeps everything in order so that life can thrive here on planet Earth. From then, my life began to change. I started to become very happy and more friendly. More loving and eager for a life minus the misery. This was the day that I left AA (Ardknocks Anonymous).

I am truly grateful for all the shit in my life. This is the manure of experience that has helped me to grow, blossom, and transform like in the same way that a caterpillar turns into a butterfly, I now have wings to fly and my old life is no more.

Glen

Time Was

There was the time I was last in the queue, for the triangles, hid at the back of the class. With the one without a strap until Miss saw me, sent me to the classroom to sit with the boys. The ones she said couldn't sing.

And the time she sent me home with my sewing, to finish all weekend; didn't ask to see it on Monday morning. The time she kept sending me, back to my desk with my posters for the summer fair. Didn't tell me how to make them better.

Then there was the time your mother made you ill. When you told her that Sunday you were going out with me, and you arrived shaken. And when she said our wedding list was like a shopping list, and had to be edited before her friends could see it. And the time she turned up at our honeymoon hotel, 'For a little break' after we'd booked an extra night. And we went home to rearrange our presents that she'd unpacked and put into our cupboards.

Then the time I moved out and you turned up, on my doorstep in a new camel coat to collect the rings. But then there was the time I got through an interview, after my hundredth application. Got on a train out of there. And the time I flew across the pond on my overdraft. Gave myself space; where the only person who knew me was me. Where I became acquainted with the bits of myself, I'd forgotten. Dropped off the bits of myself I no longer needed.

And the time I came back to start a new jigsaw of myself, with pieces that fitted together in my design.

Kathy

Together

Together we stand, together we live.
No matter where you are from, or what your sexual orientation or race is.
We are all born and all die. We all bleed.
Support each other; take care of each other.
Love not war. Happy not sad. Positive not negative.

Craig

Together, we can

Together, we can face many battles, be it of mind or body, when people support and care for each other.
Together can change laws that are not fit for purpose. As the world we live in changes, people face bias and hurt because they are different.
Together, people can bridge gaps that have developed over time by just taking time to care for their neighbours and the environment.
Together, we all breathe the same air, need food and water, warmth and love.
Together, we can do that for each other.
Together, we can change bad into good.
If everyone sticks together, anything is possible.

Marie

All be Together

Once upon a time, there was a major crime.
A virus broke the rules and shut down all the schools.
The people hid away; their boundaries couldn't stray.
The government hit hard as death was on the cards.
No smile behind the mask, our heroes were on task.
The nation did its best and yet there was unrest.
Protest in the street, with power in their feet
Unison we need. So stop neglect and greed.
Our planet is in danger from our selfish nature.
So all colours of mankind, a solution we will find.
We will find a way. It will come the day.
We will all be together. All be together.

Mel

Together we are Stronger

It takes courage to stand up and be counted. It takes real courage to speak truth to power, to stay true to our higher principles, to act and speak with real integrity, especially when those around us may not agree!

There is a Chinese proverb that says, 'He who follows the herd, ends up standing in the shit.' Think about it for a moment and consider: do I just fall in and go along with what everyone is saying, even if it makes me feel a bit uncomfortable? Do I just put up and shut up for an easy life? Or do I have the courage to stay true to myself?

I'm a big believer that we all are stronger when we find kindred spirits to rely on and align with. Because we are then able to maximise our potential to make positive changes. Encouraging people, educating people, dispelling false narratives and so-called fake news are all really important things that we can do.

Margaret Mead said, 'Never ever depend on governments or institutions to solve any major problems. All social change comes from the passion of individuals. Never doubt that a small group of thoughtful, committed citizens can change the world; indeed, it's the only thing that ever has.'

I love these words. They speak to that part of me that is inspired by social action. So yes, let's all find common ground and learn to celebrate diversity. Let's all stand tall and strong and speak truth to power. Because when we do, all things become possible. Indeed, together we really are stronger!

Terry

Train Station

Train station; renewing life in each journey.
Arriving people gaze at departing ones.
Here, life is the junction of leaving and living.
Smells of desires of each adventure.
Let's see if I can find a familiar face, or I might find faces here.
A love pilgrimage.
First, we kissed, welcome. Then we cried, will you come again?
This is our life, often farewell, whoever most we loved.
I can stay here, gazing at people on their own.
Smells of other passengers' perfume drained me in the deep ocean of yearn.
Will she come again? This scent covers my head.
Train station renewing. The floor, the roofs.
All the words are heard in loads of stories.
They heard my voice when I begged you to not leave. Stay, any time.
Frames on the walls, soldiers from old wars, a mother farewells her sons to go to war.
A frame of a bride with lace in her hair; white dress.
A soldier's lover stands behind.
They repainted the station to hide all dark history written on the surface of all walls.

Zainab

Unheard

Unheard, ignored, isolated in the room.
He stood up, his guts and voice trembled.
Stumbling words.
Flushing, avoiding eye contact.
And then, passion flowed and his face glowed,
with warmth, not nerves, embarrassment, or fear.
When he finished, a woman came over to give him a hug.
'Together, we are stronger,' she whispered.
And the world changed just a little bit.

Alan

Vessel

I didn't want an urn to hold you.
We, both queasy about cremation, but there had to be a ves-
sel to convey you.
I didn't want to browse coffin handles, muse over patinas,
veneers, for you to lie atop a rolled in trolley.
Wheeled to the very front of the chapel, where you would
never put yourself, make an exhibition of yourself.
Have to listen to your life story.
Paraded in front of the whole blessed congregation.
I just wanted you to slip into the seat next to me, grip my
hand, raise your voice to the hymns I had to choose for you.

Kathy

Walking Inspiration

Reliable, understanding, professional, and passionate,
until you meet her, you won't know the half of it.
Problem solver, kind, honest and adorable;
if it's within reason, nothing is implausible.
Now you are here, things may seem unclear.
Don't hide, or hesitate with fear.
Every time you feel that hope is gone,
Rupa will help you feel you belong.
Looking small, standing tall,
beautiful Ru, will guide us true.
Just a little over 4"10, she has the power of ten men.
Leading with elegance and class, queen-like authority,
with physical and mental health, her number one priority.
Her eyes and smile, you'll struggle to find brighter.
For every moment spent with her, leaves you feeling lighter.
She'll try her very best to take troubling times away.
The rest is up to you. Go forth, have a lovely day.

A Soul Saved

Warm Welcome

Feeling welcome is different for everyone.
We don't all sing and dance to the same song.
We are all unique in our own way.
But we can all strive to grow each day.
Loud, quiet, brash, bold.
Some like it hot, some like it cold.
When you come to Stages door,
you can forget about your life before.
Slowly, but surely, they'll get to know you well.
What lies in the future, no one can tell.
Step strong, step forward,
don't worry if you pause.
Because you'll always feel warm,
walking through Stage's doors

A Soul Saved.

Welcome

My hands greeting you, never asked for a warm return.
Skies always welcoming our prayers, tears, and dreams.
We always flew to the skies.
Dim welcoming sun, to born every night, a twilight welcoming dawn.
Thirst avidly welcoming water.
I, here, welcome your eyes to see my vision.
Deaf welcoming, a word sounds on a book as a reader.
Let's farewell the hatred to welcome the peace.
Infidel, farewell to worship God with faith.
Pens, welcoming papers to write a welcoming letter.
Snooze, welcoming our eyes to kiss the pillows.
Till tomorrow's day!
I welcome my dreams to host a crescent moon tonight.

Zainab

Welcome, my Friend

Welcome, my friend, welcome. My life is better for knowing you, and I mean that! I know you haven't always felt welcome in the past and I feel for you. I can only imagine how hard that must have been.

But there's nothing either of us can do about the past. Only the here and now is where it matters, and right here, right now, I am so glad that you have come. Tell me, my friend, about your journey. Talk to me of your life, your history, your story. I am so interested.

Let's find the common ground. Let's build those bridges. Let's heal those hurts from the past. I love to listen and I am happy to share a little of my own story should you wish to hear. And please, only share with me what you feel safe to reveal. What you do share will stay between you and I.

I am all ears, my friend. My heart is open to what you have to say. Thank you once again for coming and welcome, my friend, welcome.

Terry

What is Important?

What is important to me?
Self-respect and to respect others.
To have confidence.
To be strong in situations and be resourceful.
To be caring and supportive, and not see others struggle in life.
To be able to communicate without any hang-ups.
To be treated as I would treat others, and not be taken advantage of.
To have my own space (me time).
To accept compliments without getting embarrassed or ashamed of myself.

Julie

Art Work

Gary

Rae

Rae

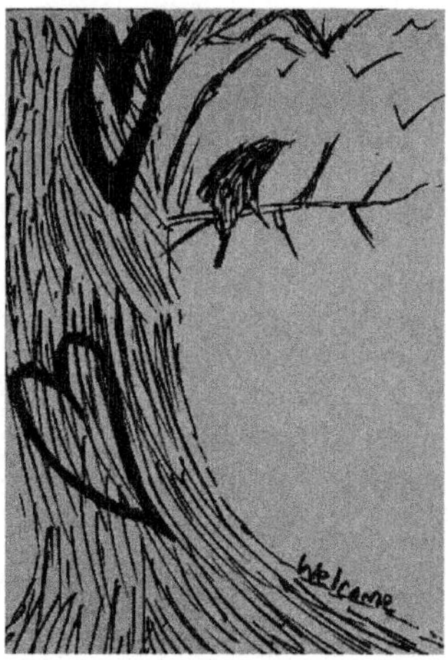

Rae

Acknowledgements

Thank you to the Ministry of Local Government, Housing and Communities, The National Lottery Community Fund, and North East and North Cumbria Integrated Care Board for funding the South Tees Changing Futures Programme. The programme has been delivered through Middlesbrough Council as lead body with delivery support from other key partners including Redcar & Cleveland Borough Council, MVDA and Beyond Housing. Significant contributions have also been made from a wide and diverse range of other partners through supporting frontline delivery and influencing future priorities for South Tees.

Thank you to colleagues and partner agencies behind the scenes who helped make this book happen, and believed that Write on the Tyne (CIC) was the right fit for such a wonderful, impactful project.

And a massive thank you to each person who submitted to this incredible collection. It was an honour to be trusted with the experiences and emotions of strangers who believed in the power and impact of sharing. Your voice is important and your words will reach many. They will empower, validate, educate, and bring joy. Thank you.

For more information visit: www.redcar-cleveland.gov.uk/community-support/south-tees-changing-futures-programme

For more information about Write on the Tyne (CIC) visit: www.writeonthetyne.com

Printed in Dunstable, United Kingdom

64078140R00077